Money 101

Learning how to make, keep and grow money!

Mantsha Pheeha

Other Books from Mantsha Pheeha

Single and Loving It

How to Pray the Word of God

Failure is not Final

How to Realise your Personal Vision

Forsaking all to follow Jesus

Website	http://www.mantsha.com
Email	Mantsha@mantsha.com
Wordpress	Mantshap
LinkedIn	Mantsha Pheeha
Facebook	mantsha.com
Twitter	@mantsha
Instagram	Mantsha Pheeha
You Tube	Mantsha Pheeha

All rights reserved. No portion of this book may be reproduced, stored in a retrieval system, or transmitted in any form or by any means—electronic, mechanical, photocopy, recording, scanning, or other—except for brief quotations in critical reviews or articles, without the prior written permission of the publisher. Published in South Africa, by Mantsha Ministries. All titles may be purchased in bulk for educational, business, fund-raising, or sales promotional use.

All Scripture quotations are taken from the New King James Version; where a different version of the Bible is used, this is indicated in the text.

Copyright © 2017 Mantsha Pheeha

ISBN- 9781973477228

Preface

I have checked my bank balance more than ten times this week. I am not sure exactly what it is that I expect to see. The bank notifies me every time when there is a deposit or withdrawal, but my phone is just quiet. The only people that keep calling me are the people I owe money. I personally think the people that work at these call centres notify each other and decide to harass me simultaneously. As soon as I pick up the phone, I hear a formal voice on the other side asking to speak to Miss Pheeha (pronounce Fihah) and then as soon as I have verified security details, the Spanish inquisition begins:

"Miss Fihah, you have not paid your account this month."

In my mind, I'm shouting: "Of course I know that I haven't paid, I don't have money!"

But in real life, I humbly respond: "Yes ma'am, I have not been able to pay."

"Is there any reason why you have not paid your account? Do you know that your credit record will be affected negatively if you do not honour your commitments with us? When are you going to pay this account? Are you aware that next month's debit order is due next week?"

I can't afford to scream. The call centre agent is just doing her job. She sounds so cold and so rude though. I wonder if she is ever unable to pay any of her debts. I must remain calm, and I do, "Ma'am, as soon as I have money I will pay the outstanding amount."

"But when will you pay ma'am?"

"I don't know sisi (sister). I don't know when I am going to get money. I don't know where the money will come from, but as soon as I get any money I will settle my account."

The woman on the other side of the phone is not happy, but I answered so matter-of-factly, she realises that there is nothing she can do. She reluctantly ends the conversation and I hang up.

I can't put a name to this feeling these kind of calls bring in me. It is a combination of despair, frustration, embarrassment, anger and disappointment. My despair and frustration come from the fact that I have no idea how long things will continue like this for me. It has been two years since I have stopped working (since I have been fired to be exact). Other than 2 months of consulting and a handful of speaking gigs, I haven't had a stable income in the two years since I left work. The decision not to look for work and to focus on business seems to make sense on most days, but every time I look at my bank balance, I wonder if that decision makes any sense at all.

I am embarrassed because with all my qualifications and work experience, and supposed brains and intelligence, I still don't have a solid plan to fund my lifestyle. In a world where I am surrounded by colleagues who are buying luxury cars, mansions and funding businesses, it is downright embarrassing to know that I do not have the R700 required to pay for my phone bill. It is embarrassing to know that I am not even resourceful enough to fund my own life, let alone fund any life changing projects.

I am angry and disappointed in myself because at 39 I am struggling with problems that belong to people who have just come out of school. What is the point of my entire working experience? If life rewards us according to the value we are adding, then clearly I am adding no value, because if I were, then life would certainly reward me.

Being broke is not just about money in my life. Being broke is about me and the contribution I am making in this world. When I am broke, I don't see properly. I see my entire life through the window of lack. It is so easy to see myself as an underachiever and a failure, and I have a feeling I'm not the only one. Money is such an amplifier. When finances are not adding up, it seems as if nothing else is working out.

In the world I come from, money problems aren't discussed. When you have money problems, you must keep quiet and resolve them alone in silence. In the very same world, being broke is embarrassing and shameful and it must be kept a secret at all cost. If you can, don't show people that you can't afford things, just find a way to make things happen and deal with the consequences later. The funny thing is no one taught us this behaviour around money. We found the people in our environment handling money this way and we just continued without asking any questions.

I'm fortunate because not having money doesn't make me feel too embarrassed. I just see it as another one of the challenges in my life that I need to overcome, and in writing this book, I hope I can assist you with your own money woes or open your eyes so that you can help those around you.

Money is important, whether you love money or not is not the issue, the reality for most of us is that every day in our lives we need money. The silence around our financial realities denies us an opportunity to have a conversation about money. There is much wisdom to be found in the experiences of others and many mistakes will be avoided, if only we could freely share our truth about personal finances.

Disclaimer: This book does not provide financial advice. It shares bluntly about money in the hope that you can begin to be honest about your money situation and if you are one of those money geniuses, so that you can freely share your wisdom with those of us who so desperately need it, but are often forced into silence. There are qualified professionals who are registered with the Financial Services Board who are qualified to give advice on your personal finances. This book is not one of those; it seeks to motivate, enlighten and inspire you to win financially.

NB: All figures that were originally in dollars are quoted in this book in South African Rand (ZAR/R) and they are adjusted for the South African reader.

Table of Contents

Other Books from Mantsha Pheeha ii
Preface iv
Table of Contents ix
1. Introduction 1
2. What is your financial status? 4
3. Busting the lies you believe about money 9
4. Create an abundance mentality 16
5. Understand how money works 25
6. Design a personal money system 32
7. Make Money 46
8. Get out of DEBT 52
9. Understand income streams 63
10. Find a Job 69
11. Start a Business 82
12. Make Passive Income 93
13. Become part of Network Marketing 99
14. Grow Money 104
15. Conclusion 106
16. About the author 107
Endnotes 108

1. Introduction

We live in a society and generation where money is the ultimate measure of success. If you have some money, organisations will invite you to motivate them and share your story in the hope that those listening can repeat what you did and have the kind of "success" that you have enjoyed. I have listened to many of those stories, with the hope that I can replicate what those people did and make my own money. I have read countless books on money. They make sense and I think to a certain extent, I have tried to apply everything those books teach. I have listened to people who have succeeded and told myself that they are no different from me. But still, they are making money and I am not; therefore, something is definitely not working.

Have you ever sat after a bad financial decision and asked yourself what happened? How did you do something so stupid? I had just received the monthly car repayment statement. I sat in my office and wondered how such a stupid decision could have been taken by such an intelligent woman.

The car repayment was R10 300 per month, excluding insurance and fuel. Every single month for the next 72 months, I was going to pay this exorbitant figure just so I can drive this car! The instalment alone would not tell you of the magnitude of the stupidity involved in purchasing this car. The real mess was hidden in the fact that I didn't even have a cent to put down as a deposit, so I had to pay for my rash decision with a whooping prime plus 4% interest rate. This car loan was more expensive than my credit card and somehow I still signed on the dotted line. In one moment of insanity, I moved from having a fully paid and fully functional car for which I paid a mere R500 in insurance monthly, to this monster of a total cost of R14 000 per month. This was my story. After reading all the financial books I had read, why would I still make this decision? Why do I forget everything I know when I have to take a decision? Why is it that when I see shoes I like, I forget everything I spent my life learning about money. I say crazy things like, "These shoes were speaking to me" or "This dress was just made for me!"

I know for a fact that I'm not the only one. It seems that there's some 'devil', waiting for an opportune moment to detract me from my journey to financial freedom. Maybe it's not the devil, maybe it's just the weaker me trying to upstage the real me when it comes to money. With the next few words, I invite you to triumph over the weaker you. I invite you to win the struggle against the part of yourself that constantly sabotages all your financial goals and dreams. You can't get rich paying for overpriced loans and you can't pay for your basic needs if you don't know how to make, keep and grow your money.

I neither have the qualification or the know-how to tell you how to make, keep and grow your money, but what we are going to do together is bust your myths and arm you with principles that will disarm the weaker you and empower the stronger you to overcome and hop on to financial breakthrough.

This first instalment of the Money Series, Money 101, will focus mainly on making and keeping money, and begin to introduce ideas around growing your money. In the discussions held throughout the book, the reader will notice that as you make and keep more money, the strategies employed will also grow your money.

2. What is your financial status?

Eternally broke: You are broke, you have always been broke and there's no light at the end of the tunnel

Some people don't have money; they have never had it and most times, they think they will never have it. Life is just strange like that. Some of us just seem to struggle. They try to go to school and either fail or can't pay the fees and never get the degree. If they do get the qualification and try to find a job, they are sentenced to a lifetime of unemployment and lack. Still, others do find jobs but they are in a permanent state of underemployment: always earning too little no matter how hard they work. When they start businesses, deals don't materialise, the business never takes off or come out of survival mode and money is forever scarce.

Has been: You once had money and now you are broke

These are the ones who had money at some point in their lives and they don't have it now. They are trying to recover and rebound but it seems that their money success was in the past and would never come to their lives again. Businesses fold, people are retrenched, contracts end, failed relationships leave you in financial ruin, and lives change forever.

More month than the money: You make money but you are always broke

No matter how much money you make, it is just never enough. You run out of money in the middle of the month and you are just one pay cheque away from utter poverty. Most times, you cannot even account for what you did with the money you received. It stresses you but it doesn't stress you enough to do something decisive and definite about it. You have learnt to work your entire life around your money situation and so far, it is working for you. You know where to borrow, how to move your money between accounts and credit cards, and on the surface you look like all is well. You are the only one that knows that if anyone can just scratch beyond your financial surface then your house of cards will come tumbling down.

Black tax (family tax)

The phrase "black tax" refers to the financial responsibility of providing for extended family. It originates from the notion that the group of people who often have to take care of extended family members are black, especially in South Africa. Since the introduction of this term, it has brought a shift in how Africans think about money. Historically, it has always been an honourable thing to take care of your extended family and even members of the community who are not related to you. Some of us may be in that place where our personal financial demands have to be carefully balanced with the needs to provide for the extended family.

Midas (golden) touch

In Greek Mythology when Midas was asked by Silenus for his choice of whatever reward he wished for after caring for Silenus, Midas asked that whatever he might touch should be changed into gold. It was a lovely experience to turn things into gold until Midas tried to eat, his food turned into gold, and he could not eat nor drink. His daughter also came rushing to him to hug him and before he could stop her, the little girl had turned into a golden statue in her daddy's arms.

The story starts well because many of us would love to have gold in abundance. Towards the end of the tale though, we realise that money is not everything and if it kills our families and denies us the peace to eat and drink merrily, then it becomes destructive in our lives. Greed, corruption and an insatiable hunger for more continues to plague our society. Many people abandon their dreams and values in a never-ending pursuit of riches and wealth, where nothing is ever enough.

Those who are so good with money

You start a business and it succeeds. You are forever climbing the ladder in your career, every investment you make doubles in return and you are on the highway to wealth and fortune. You live a balanced life and we all wish to have your wisdom.

The disciplined person

These people work hard, get promotions and increases, and maybe have a side business, but in the main, they can afford the basics in life and a few luxuries now and then.

The imposter

Everyone thinks you have a lot of money but you are broke as hell.

The invisible

You grew up poor and now you have money and everyone thinks you are still poor. No one ever asks for your opinion, let alone for any kind of financial contribution.

These categories show us that we are all dealing with money from a different point of view. Our point of view is like a coloured glass through which we see everything being discussed in this book. That coloured glass will distort the colour of everything that you see. When it comes to money, it is almost impossible to be objective because you see money based on where you come from, where you are and where you wish to go. When you understand what your financial status is, then you are able to self-correct when you find yourself being too defensive, sceptical, dismissive, angry or even overwhelmed as you read this book.

These ideas can work in the life of anyone who is willing to apply them, they don't discriminate. Don't convince yourself that money is not for you.

3. Busting the lies you believe about money

Passion and money

How often have I heard these words: "Follow your passion, and the money will follow" or "Do what you love and the money will follow." I am following my passion, I am doing what I love so where is the money? Some people are fortunate that the thing they are passionate about generates income but for most of us, our passions are often not aligned to our income ambitions. Just because you have to do something else to make money, doesn't mean you have to abandon your passion. This means you can still pursue a passion that doesn't make the type of money your lifestyle needs, whilst at the same time, you are pursuing moneymaking activities that are not related to your passion.

It is also important to consider that most people may not get the opportunity to make money in the area of their passion early in life. But as you get older, opportunities will open up for you to commit fully to your passion and to not have to work on separate income-generating activities. I have seen many people who abandoned their income-generating activities to follow their passions, struggling to make ends meet. It may be worthwhile that if you are feeling the pull and pressure of your passion, to consider waiting a few months or even years, which will make the entire experience more enjoyable for you and your family.

A job is the only way to have money

A job is not the only way to make money.

There are other ways of making money that are different from traditional employment and the main thing that makes them so scary is the fact that most of us don't understand them well. We must all educate ourselves about the different streams of income when we are still in school, so that upon graduation from school, we can understand what other options we may have if finding a job is difficult.

Money doesn't affect my dreams

I was watching the Oprah Winfrey Show in the early 2000s and she was interviewing a talented woman who made scrapbooks. I didn't really understand the concept of scrapbooks but everyone was in awe and so was I! Apparently, scrapbooks are popular in America but here in Africa, they were not quite a thing – music books maybe, but definitely not scrapbooks. Oprah spent a considerable amount of time going through her work and the audience kept clapping and smiling throughout.

At some point, Oprah asked the woman: "Why don't you devote more time to your hobby so that you can turn it into a business?"

The woman paused and then she said: "I have to work because I have just bought a couch." At that point, the camera showed us a picture of her living room, and there it was… the brown couch, that looked old and beat down.

Oprah paused, the woman was quiet and then Oprah broke the silence and said: "You are not pursuing your dream because of this couch." In typical dramatic television style, the screen stayed on that ugly couch.

The woman nodded and said she had to work two jobs just to make payments for that couch and as soon as she finished paying it off, she would then consider a scrapbook business.

I don't remember what else happened in that episode of the Oprah Winfrey Show, but I remember very clearly how it made me feel. At first, I was just so angry. How can a person put her entire life on hold because of a couch? I mean, can an ugly sofa really stand in the way of all your dreams? A few years later, when I considered the woman's dilemma, I realised that my life was no different from hers. I also couldn't leave my job to go and preach because I was paying for the car, the house, the credit cards, and everything else that I considered a necessity at that time.

I frowned at this woman's decisions but they were no different from mine. I had signed five years of my life to pay for my car, parallel to that, another twenty years to pay off my small house, and then add to that an infinite amount of time required to pay off credit cards, clothing accounts, overdrafts, and all other credit facilities that I kept using the minute I paid the minimum required by the credit provider.

I had convinced myself that money was not important to me, that I lived my life without much care about the role of money. But on that day, I realised that money was bullying me into a life I did not choose, simply because I did not respect it enough to plan for it.

I decided to change. Being an engineer, I realised that I must devote time to learn how to make, keep and grow money. I had been an A-student in school and a struggling engineering student, but none of the courses I ever attended taught me about money. I had completed a BSc in Chemical Engineering, which I personally consider the most difficult course on earth, at, what was at that time, the best university in Africa. I had learnt complex things like Mass Balance, designed monstrosities called Heat Exchangers, attended an entire course on Corrosion and still in all my education, I hadn't learnt about money. At that point in my life, I realised that my lack of education about money, was really putting my dreams on hold. I don't know about you, but where I went to school, Money Management 101 wasn't offered. Instead, we learned about the War of 1812, which of course is something I use every single day.

Objects vs. money

If you stay at a certain place and drive a certain car, have a particular job or work for a specific company or industry, then you have money. If you live a particular lifestyle (maybe you are a turn up queen or you always hang out with rich people in specific places) then you have money.

Sometimes all the objects you have are just telling the world of your liabilities and your regular payments, but they say nothing about the amount of money you have. In some cases though, they testify of your buying power because you need some kind of income to be able to make higher purchases, but in most cases they say nothing about how much money you have. In some cases, the people with the most things are the poorest.

Education & career vs. money

If you have no formal education you don't have money, whereas if you are a graduate you do; or even better, the more you study the more money you make.

Sometimes the most educated people are the poorest amongst us. In Thomas Stanley and William Danko's book, *The millionaire next door*, the authors' biggest findings was that the people that had money were the most unlikely people. It was the people who were not as educated as you and I would have assumed. What struck me about those findings is that the blue-collar worker doesn't have to keep up appearances. The more educated you are, somehow you feel the need to stay in a certain neighbourhood, drive a particular car and dress a certain way, whereas a mechanic doesn't care much about image and can therefore save money quicker than a professor with a PhD.

To make money you need money

So many people will tell you that they can't start businesses because they need capital. As a society, we have elevated money to the point that sometimes we block all our creative juices with money limitations. Some of us have a view that access to money will change everything about our lives and answer all our problems. This type of thinking prevents us from thinking about different alternatives to fund the things we want to achieve. Students who don't go to school because they have no money allow money to blind them from the options that are available to them: bursaries, scholarships, working your way through school, part time studies while you hold a permanent job, etc. I, for one, worked, tutored, had a tuck shop, was involved in projects, sold things and had a bursary and scholarship just so I could put myself through school.

Background and money

If you are part of a particular race or family, you will have money. If your parents are rich or educated then you will have money. After a while, we all learn that our backgrounds can give us a head start, but the rest is up to us.

4. Create an abundance mentality

I went to the shelter today, and if I hadn't been so hungry, it would have been just like any other visit to the women and children's shelter (a place where women who have nowhere to stay can live temporarily whilst they got back on their feet). The housemother offered to make breakfast for me but because I want my eggs done a particular way, I insisted on making the eggs myself. She opened the pantry for me and told me to get the foodstuffs I needed to prepare my breakfast. I think I spent about ten minutes in total wonder, that pantry looked like a Woolworths store. I couldn't believe it, this is a place where people who have nowhere to go, stay and their pantry is full of a wealthy person's supply of all the exotic food you can think of. I kept asking if they eat the stuff, if they had any idea how good it is, how expensive it all is. I tried to explain that I simply couldn't afford most of it and the housemother just laughed it all off.

To the naked eye, all you see is women who have reached such a low in their lives that they live in the shelter, but actually, those women eat like kings, and they didn't even know it. An abundance mentality is not about how much money you have, it sees provision as something greater than money. As the women sit in that shelter wishing to leave and praying every day for jobs and for houses they can rent, they don't realise that even though it is not the way they would have preferred, God has found a different way to provide for them.

Imagine a person with a glass of water in a river. That person may look at the water in the glass and think "I have a bit of water" or he may choose to look at the entire river and realise that he has access to all the water in the river. All he has to do is draw as much as he wants. It is how you see and not what you see that really matters. Even when we say that there is a depression or the economy is not doing well, we still see other people prospering. In the economy, one person can get a better job and in the very same economy, another person can be retrenched or fail to get a job.

Most people are quick to conclude that there is a shortage and that we live in a world of not enough: not enough jobs, money, etc. If we are to make a difference in our lifetime, then we must see clearly and understand that there is abundance. We must not focus too much on what we see, but rather focus on ourselves.

Recently, when I was complaining about the fact that I haven't bought myself clothes in a long time, a friend made me realise that I always get dresses and shoes as gifts. A scarcity mentality sees that I haven't bought clothes but an abundance mentality sees the access to dresses and shoes and bags bought all over the world that I may not have had the money to buy, even if I had money. An abundance mentality is a mind-set, the very same way that a scarcity mentality is a mind-set, and it is not changed by whether you currently have money or not.

A scarcity mentality thinks the pie is not big enough for all of us, but an abundance mentality thinks of ways to increase the pie so all of us can have a share. A scarcity mentality always sees the shortage and wants to grab as much as possible, whereas an abundance mentality knows that there is always a way to make room for one more person and therefore, is as generous as possible. Examine yourself and ask yourself, "do I possess an abundance or a scarcity mentality?"

In the Millionaire Next Door, the authors proved to the world that ordinary people became millionaires by the habits they built on what most of us would consider an average income. When you possess an abundance mentality, you don't allow your level of income to convince you that you can't do well with money.

Provision is greater than money

If a person is travelling to the village and he is praying for transport money to go home, the expectation is that God will answer with money. Instead of receiving money, there is another person who is also going home and he offers the traveller a lift home, free. The person asked for money and they would have had to travel to the taxi rank, catch a taxi, pay for it and be dropped somewhere else and finally, walk home. The answer the traveller got is much better, because the person offering the lift will go to the traveller's house, pick him up and then take him straight to his homestead in the village. The traveller never received money, but what he got instead was so much more than money and it cannot even be quantified in rand or dollars.

Most people are focused so much on what they do not have, that they never get to see and celebrate all the things they have. I will give you a few examples from my own life. I exercise at least three times every single week and that earns me smoothies from my medical aid. When I count the income in my life, I never count those smoothies, but just because they are free for me doesn't mean no one is paying for them. I generally work at Starbucks because they have free Wi-Fi and again I don't spend lots of money buying data, but just because I'm not paying for the Wi-Fi doesn't mean it costs nothing. Sometimes I attend seminars and they give us free lunch or when I'm speaking and I get my travel and lodging paid for in places that others consider holiday destinations. I don't count all of that when I consider my income but the truth is, they are part of God's way of bringing provision into my life. This concept applies to something as simple as attending a funeral, wedding, party or service where they provide you with food without asking you to pay, or visiting a family or friend and they feed you or give you something to drink. These examples are crazy but just look at your past month, year or week and look at all the little pleasures that God brought your way that you never acknowledged or celebrated.

Before you are so quick to think about just how broke you are, rather look at the real truth. You are alive, which means you haven't starved to death. You somehow managed to get hold of this book, which means you are more resourceful than you are willing to give yourself credit. Having an abundance mentality will teach you to be more grateful and to complain less; you will pursue your goals from a place of peace and not of panic or despair.

Funding your basic needs is the lowest form of provision

It's very important to understand that your basic needs are taken care of so that you can focus on making money to fund your dreams. If you are too caught up in where your next meal is going to come from, you will not have the time or capacity to focus on your dreams and future. *Jeremiah 12:5 says: " If you have run with the footmen, and they have wearied you, then how can you contend with horses? And if in the land of peace, In which you trusted, they wearied you, then how will you do in the floodplain of the Jordan?"* Focusing only on your basic needs is the same as running with footmen and living in the land of peace. But if you want to do more, to fund great things, to set yourself apart, then we liken you to the one contending with horses or living in the flooded land. If you are so concerned about your basic needs, they tend to cloud you and you can't think beyond bread, shelter and water.

When you think big, then the small things will take care of themselves. This type of thinking is difficult when you are struggling with the basic things, but once you force yourself to think of dreams and to think of your future, then you will not wait for things to be well financially before you pursue your purpose.

Remove worrying about money from your life

Worrying about money does not produce any change, except if that worry results in action. Even in that case, it is not the worrying that produces the results, it is the action. When you worry about money, you accomplish nothing and by now, most of us know that worrying did not change our situation one bit. Sometimes, when things are really bad, utilities get cut off, assets gets repossessed or interest payments skyrocket, we believe that we can't help but worry.

The Bible promises us that these things will be taken care of and somehow, even the most committed Christian just doesn't get it when things are rough financially. Let us look at the verses:

Matthew 6:25 "Therefore I say to you, do not worry about your life, what you will eat or what you will drink; nor about your body, what you will put on. Is not life more than food and the body more than clothing? 26 Look at the birds of the air, for they neither sow nor reap nor gather into barns; yet your heavenly Father feeds them. Are you not of more value than they? 27 Which of you by worrying can add one cubit to his stature? 28 "So why do you worry about clothing? Consider the lilies of the field, how they grow: they neither toil nor spin; 29 and yet I say to you that even Solomon in all his glory was not arrayed like one of these. 30 Now if God so clothes the grass of the field, which today is, and tomorrow is thrown into the oven, will He not much more clothe you, O you of little faith? 31 "Therefore do not worry, saying, 'What shall we eat?' or 'What shall we drink?' or 'What shall we wear?' 32 For after all these things the Gentiles seek. For your heavenly Father knows that you need all these things. 33 But seek first the kingdom of God and His righteousness, and all these things shall be added to you.34 Therefore do not worry about tomorrow, for tomorrow will worry about its own things. Sufficient for the day is its own trouble.

When your bank account is empty or you don't have access to cash, it is very easy to worry about the things the Bible tells us not to worry about. The instruction is clear here, we cannot worry about food, a place to stay, or clothes, but how many of us worry all the time? Worrying is unbiblical. The absence of money in your account is not a passport to 'worryville'. Even when there is no money, the Bible still says we must not worry. Worry will paralyse you. Instead of working on income-generating projects, worry will keep you busy and you will stay in a rut longer than you should.

I know what it's like to not know where money for food will come from. I know how it feels to drive a car on reserve when you don't have money to fill up. I have experienced the despair of watching your toiletries and cleaning products disappear right in front of your eyes. Bouncing debit orders and endless calls from creditors… I have experienced it all. One thing that I can tell you for sure is that worrying never changed any of it. All the time you spend worrying is time taken away from something more productive like coming up with ideas of how to make money, getting work done, etc. Worry is a thief, and any second you spend worrying is time lost forever, never to be recovered.

Poverty, lack and being broke, is mostly a mind-set more than a state of being. Those with a scarcity mentality are quick to notice what they need and what they do not have. Those with an abundance mentality always begin from a place of acknowledging what they have, even if it cannot be measured in money. The mind-set will then determine how you pursue making and keeping money. The one with the scarcity mentality will always come from a place of not enough, always feeling left behind and chasing an imaginary deadline. Whereas those with the abundance mentality will always come from a place where the pie is big enough for everyone, therefore, their efforts are steadier and are pursued from a place of peace.

Money is not a destination; it is a means to get to the destination. The destination could be ownership or access. Instead of focusing on the means rather focus on the destination, because you may already have in your possession the very thing you want money to buy for you.

So in this chapter, we need to settle the fact that God will take care of our basic needs: food, shelter and clothing. If it appears as if we do not have any of these things, then we go to God and ask for His provision. This will also help us to deal with any greed, gluttony or a desire to show off to others. Here God is taking care of everything that He knows we need and the rest of our time and energy, where money is concerned, will be for other things… much bigger things!

5. Understand how money works

The history of money

Money is a medium of exchange. In ancient days, when the economy was based solely on farming and hunting, people needed to find a way to fairly exchange their goods and services. When the onion farmer wanted to buy a cow from the cattle farmer, one cow was equivalent to 40 bags of onions, but the cattle farmer only needed one bag of onions for the entire month. On the other hand, when the orange farmer was ready to exchange his oranges for apples, he found that the apple farmer could not exchange yet because his apples were not yet ready for harvest. In order to deal with this challenge of quantities and timing, the farmers came up with a system of writing "I owe you" notes, which indicated that they could pay each other beyond the moment of exchange.

If the onion farmer needed a cow but the cattle farmer did not need onions, then the onion farmer would take the cow in exchange for a note that indicated that the onion farmer is indebted to the cattle farmer until such time that both farmers could find a suitable form of exchange. The process was tedious and it was difficult to determine the true cost of goods and services, so money was introduced as a standard form of exchange for all goods and services.

You knew the true cost of a bag of onions regardless of whether you farmed cattle, oranges or apples. Thus, money in its different forms was introduced into our society. Money was simple back then, people were not trying to become rich or hoard all the cash. People wanted to buy goods and services for their everyday lives, and they were content.

The 'new' meaning of money

Somewhere along the way, money morphed and turned into something it was never intended to be. Now, money is seen as a symbol of power and success. People use it to oppress and lord over each other. Others even use it to determine the worth of a person, and in some religious circles, the blessing of God is measured in money.

These new-found meanings of money have also resulted in a number of instruments being created to entertain the greed and insatiable hunger for money. Money is no longer just a means of exchanging goods and services, it is considered a status symbol and many have devoted their entire lives to its pursuit.

On the other hand though, the absence of money in a person's life can lead to all kinds of misfortune and misery. Without money you have no food or shelter, you cannot visit the doctor when you are sick, and you cannot even take your children to school. It appears that our whole world is run by money. It is therefore important to know how to make, or rather, how to get money.

Who taught you about money?

Our education prepares us for many things, but it doesn't really teach us how to make money. Money is so important in our society, yet there is not a single class in our primary and high schooling careers that directly focuses on teaching leaners to make money. For most people, mathematics is considered a difficult subject. Unfortunately, it is the same subject that makes up the foundation for handling money.

At the root of most problems that people have with money, is a lack of understanding mathematical principles. In order to have money to save, invest, give or spend, you must first make money. Basic mathematics should make it obvious to each of us that if there is no income, then we cannot even begin to discuss investments, savings, etc.

Most of us understand one form of making money well… the salary. The salary is generally so predictable and easy to understand, and we have spent so much time studying it that we all subconsciously find security in knowing that we receive it. All countries track employment numbers and use those statistics to measure the wellbeing of a country's economy. So, it is no wonder that even individuals measure their success according to whether or not they have a job, and how much money they make from that job.

If the schooling system is not designed to teach us about money, then where does the average person learn about money? In most households, discussions about money are not an everyday occurrence. The average family will only talk about money when it is needed and they will not invest any additional time into talking about the acquisition and accumulation of money. In our social circles, discussions about money are often limited to hot topics and unfounded tales, so those discussions do not provide the foundational principles needed to understand how money works.

In recent times, there has been a wide variety of writings about money, which is our society's attempt to contribute positively to the discussion about money. There is endless literature about money. However, we must caution the reader because some of the literature is based on hype and the drive to sell. On the other hand, there is also very good literature that if applied can assist each of us to be successful with money.

A new way of thinking about money

When you are at school, someone makes it their business to design the entire curriculum for your school career. From the time you walk into grade zero, to the time you exit the schooling system in grade twelve, there is a well-planned path complete with lessons, exams, assignments, tests, homework, quizzes, etc. At school, we are told when to arrive at school and when to leave, when to eat, and even when we go to the bathroom, we ask for permission. This conditioning doesn't bade well for some of us when we leave school. When there is no one to tell us what to do, we fail to take the initiative and manage our own lives.

The reason why many of us enter our adulthood focused solely on getting a job, is mainly because a full-time job still maintains the same security we had at school. In a conventional job there is still someone telling us when to arrive at work and when to leave, when to eat lunch or have a tea break. Even performance contracts are drafted in a way that someone else designs our jobs for us. We just have to deliver and our salaries will follow us at a set time every single month or week. A job is the closest thing we have after school that is like school, and because man is a creature of habit, we seek a job so that we can continue with what we know.

There are 'other' streams of income, but they are so different from what we are used to, they require a different way of thinking. The qualities needed to develop a new stream of income must be learnt from scratch. The birth of a business, freelancing, contracting or temporary work is so foreign to the school leaver because it is so different from the system we know. Most of us would rather not get involved. The fear of the unknown keeps us from developing new income streams.

Making money is not limited to a job or a salary; there is more to making money than that. In order to explore all there is to making money, we need to immediately remove this limited way of thinking.

Your next steps

This book provides an introduction to some principles about money. This book is meant to stimulate your thinking and interest so that you can decide to become a student of money. In dealing with the different topics that this book introduces, the author will not exhaust all the options, as this would result in a very large volume that may be too big for any reader to be interested in.

As you read about the different streams of income, for example, please conduct your own research. In the different chapters, one example will be discussed in depth and the rest will be left to the reader's own research. The word research may appear intimidating for some people, but what it simply means is to find different sources of information and then decide on the best option for yourself. Your research may include speaking to people who are successful with money, reading biographies of people who have succeeded in your stream of choice, reading articles, online searches using your smartphone or computer, attending seminars and workshops, attending short courses, etc.

Don't be stuck in analysis paralysis or in stirring the ocean; this is where your research is endless and you never get to a point where you implement your learning. Don't try to look for the best option, because it doesn't exist; just pick a course, and commit to it. Making money is not a result of much studying but of consistent doing. Get started. Commit to starting as soon as you finish reading this book. If it takes you 3 days to finish reading this book, then by the end of day three, pick one stream of income and start working on it immediately.

The power of this book is not in the information that is contained in it, but its power is in the reaction of the reader to its contents. The author seeks to stir the reader to get up and be systematic and consistent about making, keeping and growing money. Once you are done with this book, get up and make money. Make it and keep it, then grow it.

6. Design a personal money system

As human beings, we unknowingly use systems every single day. For example, everyone has a hygiene system that involves daily activities like brushing teeth, bathing or taking a shower, applying lotion, using bath soap, some kind of facial routine and hair-care practice, etc. One person chooses to take a shower and another takes a bath, both persons will be clean and no one activity is better than the other is. We choose different products based on preference, sensitivity, type of skin, etc. Without realising it, we took decisions over time and ultimately decided to choose an optimal system based on the conclusions we made over a certain period.

There are other systems that we use like nutrition, which include food preparation, grocery shopping, dining out, etc. We also have systems that cover our careers, relationships, etc. Each of us also has a money system that we have developed, but for the average person, that money system came by default and there was very little thought that went into designing it. At this point, it may be worthwhile for you to think about how you came about your personal money system and what activities are included in that system.

These few questions can assist you to get going in thinking about your personal system:

- What informs the way you think about money: Is it fear, past lack, seeing the success of others, your dreams?
- What are your money habits: Do you save, spend every cent that hits your account, use credit as a lifestyle, make many regret purchases?
- What is your internal outlook about money: are you disciplined, are you so stingy that you never enjoy your money, are you anxious that you will never have money success, are you paralysed or can you make the necessary money moves you need for financial victory?

Reflecting on these and other questions will assist you to analyse the origin of your current money system. An additional step to take would be to quickly analyse if your current money system is working for you. Is your current system giving you sustainable success? Do you like the results of the activities you are currently engaged in? If your responses are favourable, then it may be worthwhile to take a few minutes and write down your system in detail so that you can pass it on to others in your life. If you are not happy with the results, then read on so that you can find ways to create a new money system that will produce different results.

The fundamentals of a good money system

Firstly, a good money system must have at least three parts: 1) making money, 2) keeping money and finally, 3) growing money.

These three parts are all important and I am sure that most of us have tales of people who made money and just couldn't keep it or maybe those who kept their money, but were so miserable trying to cling to every cent because they didn't know how to grow what they had. In order to enjoy what money can do, you have to be a student of all three elements: make, keep and grow money at all times, no matter where you start or how low a base you have.

Secondly, a good system is not affected by personal circumstances or the environment. This 3-part system will work regardless of the economic climate or popular belief. The system doesn't care that you currently have nothing or that you are at below zero; the system will even work for a person who is already doing well financially. No matter where you are with your finances, you can make more money, keep more of the money you make or grow the money that you have. Initially, this is a linear 3-step process, where you first make money in order to keep it because you cannot keep what you don't have in the first place. And it is only after you have kept some money that you actually have something to grow.

To the fast learner, it may appear that this section is full of repetition, but it is important to note that, as per the Pareto Principle; personal finance is 80% behaviour and 20% knowledge. Repetition is the one thing that helps us change behaviour. Repetition is how bad habits are broken and good ones are created. No matter what I go through in life or how tough things get, I will always remember that one plus one is two because my grade one teacher drilled it into my head through repetition. The greatest step to winning with money is changing behaviour and a system will automate change in behaviour.

Thirdly, your personal finance system must speak to your core values. As human beings we are all guided by a set of values, we may not be aware, but our values provide the compass for our decisions and behaviour. If you have a 'don't care' attitude, a closer look will reveal that it comes from a set of values that you may have adopted unaware. A behaviour that includes overspending may really be a symptom of how much you value the opinion of others about you. You need to make sure that your personal money system is aligned to your values, if not, you will not be able to commit to it sustainably. The other reason why your money system must be aligned to your values is because when things get tough, you will be able to keep going because your values will give you the perseverance you need. A system will provide you with the hardwiring you need to automate the implementation of your values. If you are funding your dream, then as part of your system include a portion from all income that will go towards saving for that dream. For me as a Christian, giving is a priority and it is evident that giving is at the top of the system I use.

There is no such thing as a perfect system, just pick one and follow it. Don't straddle between the different systems, as you will struggle to see results. Please take the time and write your chosen system down. If you think that you will just keep the system in your head, remember, the reason we all need a personal money system is because it will automate our behaviour about money. Don't just follow the system in your head, even if it is your own unique design. Make sure you write it down and put it in an accessible place so that it can direct you when your impulsive and weaker self wants to take over. We will discuss five systems to manage your money in this chapter. All of them are effective, you just have to pick one and follow it with intensity and focus.

Again, it is important to choose one money system and commit to it. You can never find such a thing as a perfect system to handle your finances. What you need is a reasonable system that you can commit to for the long term. The challenge with most people is they are never consistent. Whilst working on a system, someone comes and tells them how successful they have been in a different system and they immediately abandon the system they are working on. You can never have success if you don't give the system a chance to yield results and you will always complain that nothing ever works out for you financially.

All the systems can work; what matters is not the formula behind the system, but the person implementing the system. The one thing that makes the system powerful is the fact that you make a decision once. You make the decision when you choose the system to follow. You don't have to make the decision every single time you receive money. Whether you receive a salary, an inheritance, a tax refund or a bonus, you already know what percentage to allocate where. Stick to your system of choice and it will help you reach your financial destination.

My personal system (10-10-10-70)

1. Giving (10%)
2. Long-term savings (10%) for retirement, endowment policies, investments, bonds and insurance for chronic illness, life and disability.
3. Saving for opportunities (10%) including large purchases, paying off (not down) debts and putting money aside for business opportunities. In business, this is referred to as the war chest. This is money that you put aside for going to war. There's nothing as sad as seeing an opportunity and not having the money to grab it.
4. Live on the rest (70%), covering taxes, food, shelter, transport, utilities, education, vacations, etc. This category also includes the monthly repayments that you are making on your debts and it is different from the money you are using in 3. to pay off your debt.

This system must be implemented in parallel; you start where you are and immediately allocate all your income as per the percentages indicated. At first, you may be short on the living expenses, but the change that this system brings is in the accumulation of the 30% in steps 1-3. For those of us who are starting out with zero savings, it is our opportunity to set ourselves up for a different kind of life. The most powerful thing with using percentages versus using absolute numbers is that you can start anywhere, regardless of what your level of income is. If you currently have no income then your most important objective is to get an income. As soon as you secure an income then you start with dividing that income the moment it lands in your hands.

As you get increases and bonuses, the first 10% will increase automatically, but you must work on your formula to ensure that the 70% keeps decreasing and the third 10% keeps increasing. The third 10% is the tool you will use to build your wealth as you keep getting bonuses, increases, making better sales, getting tax refunds, etc. It must grow as a percentage with proper goals.

This system, like all the other systems that I will introduce only works when you have an income, so the first thing you need to do is get an income. Don't despair as you read if you are unemployed or if your business is not making money, focus on getting an income and in time you will have numbers to feed into the system.

Dave Ramsey's Money Makeover[1]

1. Save R1 000 fast. In his book, Dave encourages the reader to find any means possible to save the money within a short space of time. If you can't find the money, he even advices that you find things to sell. Some of us are emotionally attached to things that

---

[1] Adapted from "The Total Money Makeover" by Dave Ramsey

have a monetary value and we are not willing to sell them even when we are drowning in debt.

2. Pay off all your debts except the house. He introduces a system called the debt snowball, which focuses on paying off the lowest debt (regardless of interest rate charges). You need to have gazelle like focus and intensity, and in his experience, he notes that most people would have paid off all their debts, including the car, in a period of 18 to 36 months.
3. Save 3-6 months' worth of expenses (if your expenses are R5 000 a month, it means you save between R15 000 and R30 000)
4. Maximise your retirement savings. If you speak to a reputable financial planner, you will be able to determine how much money you need to save in order to retire comfortably.
5. Fund your children's tertiary education. If you have no children, you may skip this one.
6. Pay off your house.
7. Build wealth.
8. Live a life of giving.

Dave Ramsey's system is a linear step-by-step process, which means you start with step number one and follow the steps until you reach step 8. This system needs focus because you can't move to step 3 until you have paid off all your debts. Most people may struggle to stay in step 2 for 36 months, but once you have paid off every single debt including your car, you will be in a totally different place financially. Imagine receiving your income and having no debt payments at all, your life will change and you will go through the remaining 6 steps in a flash.

5 Laws of Gold by George Clason[2]

1. Save a minimum of 10%.
2. Find opportunities to grow your money.
3. Invest your money under the guidance of qualified persons.
4. Do not invest in businesses or purposes with which you are not familiar or which are not approved by skilful people.
5. Do not force impossible earnings.

In a nutshell, George Clason is simply saying save 10% and invest wisely. Losing your savings is one of the reasons why some people's money growing activities never yield any results. If saving money is likened to planting and growing a tree, then your savings are the seeds you put into the ground. As the money grows, the seed sprouts and a small shrub begins to grow. Every time you lose money in pyramid schemes, hot unfounded schemes or premature investments, you pull your shrub out by its roots and the tree dies. You will always start from scratch if you don't allow your tree to grow. There will always be people that need help, but make sure that you don't use your savings for those needs. Keep your objectives for saving in front

---

[2] Adapted from The Richest Man in Babylon by George S. Clason

of you at all times. Retirement savings must not be used to service debt, and money in your home loan account (if you have an access bond) must not be taken out to deposit a car.

7 Cures to a lean purse by George Clason[3]

1. Save 10% of your income.
2. Control your expenditure through a budget.
3. Grow your savings.
4. Protect your savings from loss.
5. Own your house; pay off your home loan quickly or buy your house cash.
6. Build your retirement savings.
7. Find creative ways to earn more money.

This system adds two main things to George Clason's previous 5-step system, retirement savings and paying off the house. Retirement savings are very difficult to commit to because most of us think we will never get old. Being old always looks far away until it is too late. Most of us cannot imagine that there will be a time when we may not be able to make money. Old age creeps on you unaware, sickness may bring old age earlier than you thought or your career may take a turn for the worst very late in life, in such a way that you are not able to recover. Most of us always think we have more time to save for

---

[3] Adapted from The Richest Man in Babylon by George S. Clason

retirement but we don't. Money needs time to grow and you must give your retirement savings a chance to grow.

Very few purchases will affect your cash flow more than the house; 20, 25 or 30 years is the common period for paying off your home loan and this would result in you paying the original price many times over. There are many debates around the home loan as a vehicle to purchase a house, but for many people, a house is a basic need and not necessarily an investment. If we agree that we are purchasing a basic need of shelter and that many people do not have the upfront money required to buy a house cash, then we could conclude that a home loan gives access for most buyers. Now that you have a home loan, then you need to work hard to ensure that you pay it off as quickly as possible, to reduce both your interest rate and the repayment period. The purpose for this point is to free the home loan repayment so that you can use it for other things that are aligned to your values.

Napoleon Hill's Think and Grow Rich[4]

1. Decide how much money you want.
2. What activities (work or business) will you commit to, to get that money?
3. How long (exact date) will it take you to get the money?

---

[4] Adapted from Think and Grow Rich by Napoleon Hill

4. Create a definite plan to get that money, and begin at once, whether you are ready or not, to put this plan into action.
5. Write out a clear, concise statement of the amount of money you intend to acquire, name the time limit for its acquisition, state what you intend to give in return for the money, and describe clearly the plan through which you intend to accumulate it.
6. Keep reading your statement and have faith.

Napoleon Hill deals more with your mind-set. You can never be successful with money if you don't believe and think you can. His focus is on the acquisition of money and he describes a process that you can apply to make money. We must not be too caught up on how we make money per se i.e. a job, a business, freelance work, selling, etc. In point number two, you have to decide what you will do to make the money you desire. This process applies to your regular and once-off activities. This will also assist most people to consider what can be done instead of spending all their time explaining why it is not possible to make money. When I sell books, I have to decide how much money I want to make and then calculate how many books at what profit I have to sell. This applies to overtime, network marketing, an extra job, etc.

Bringing it all together

I have provided a few examples of systems that you can use and the onus is on you to decide to take one and run with it, research further or create your own combination. The trick is to pick a course and stick to it. The ingredients of a good personal finance system are that it does 3 basic things: **make, grow** and **keep** money, in line with your **values** in all **conditions**. That sounds so simple and any of us can do that.

1. Make money (work on your mind set about making money, decide on the activities you will engage in to make money: work, business, network marketing, selling, etc.).
2. Keep money (decide on a percentage to save, use a budget as a tool to control your expenses, and lower/eliminate your debt).
3. Grow the money (decide on the vehicle you will use to grow your money, automate the way you invest and be consistent).
4. Evaluate all your decisions based on your values (I do hope you have values).
5. Test your system; does it work under all conditions?

Just like that, your system is set up in five easy steps. Anyone, regardless of education, background and experience, can do this. It is simple and it requires one decision upfront. You can review your decision occasionally but in the main, just work on implementing the system you choose. We always make our best decisions based on where we are and as we grow, we can make better decisions. Don't look down on the decisions of today in the hope that you can make better decisions tomorrow. What you have is today and it is the only guarantee you have. With the benefit of hindsight, most of us can see the weaknesses of our past decisions; don't allow that to paralyse you and stop you from making your money-move now. At this point in your life, you are ready to choose a system, just do it.

7. Make Money

Most books that I have read about money assume that we are all making money. Before we continue our discussion about how you must handle your money, I want to discuss the fact that you must get money into your hands.

Is your life profitable?

In business, we talk about profit. Even in your personal life, the same principle of profit applies. In business: Profit = Income - Costs.

From the time we are born we have both income and costs; just because no one is keeping score does not mean both do not exist in our lives. Imagine if we kept score of the flow of money in our lives the way we kept score of our birthdays, where sometimes first time parents are even keeping score of days and months.

"My baby is 3 days old."

"He is turning 6 weeks tomorrow."

"She will be two in a week." We just know it means two years because we are all keeping score. We all know what a two-year-old child is supposed to look like, and very few people would make the mistake of thinking it meant two days, weeks or months when the child is actually two years old.

We also keep score of the development of the child and we have made it an integral part of our conversations and lifestyle.

"How old is she? Shouldn't she be walking already? Mine was walking already at this age!"

If the development is too slow, we panic and take the child to the doctor and all kinds of specialists. If it is too fast, then we brag and tell anyone who would listen. "Oh we are raising such a little genius, he is only 6 months old and he is walking already!"

We keep score of what we think is important when we raise children, but for some reason we only keep score of how profitable our lives are too late in life. For many of us, by the time we need to understand money in our personal lives the subject is too intimidating because it was never part of our conversations.

From the time you were born, the profitability equation applied from day one. To be precise, it applied before day one, but for the purposes of this book, we will limit its application from your first day on earth.

Baby you: Profit = Income - Costs

Income examples: Gifts from your mother's baby shower, a portion of the salaries of your parents, grandparents, guardians, etc. From the government, in the form of medical, infrastructure and birth registration expenses. Energy from your parents breastfeeding you, bathing you etc. All these things can be reduced to a rand amount, so they must be accounted for as income into your life.

Costs examples: clothes, diapers, food, medicine, etc.

For most babies, your profit is zero, and it is perfectly fine for you as a child to score zero because there's no expectation that you should be making money at the age of three. The point I wish to raise here is that beyond a certain point, you must start making money and that Profit Section of your equation must be greater than zero and keep increasing for the rest of your life. If you are silently saying: "Surely there's more to life than making money or I'm not even interested in making money" please hold that thought because we are coming to it shortly.

Are you tracking your progress when it comes to money?

As described earlier around the development of our children, we have defined and accepted norms around development and achievement. These norms are defined because there have been many studies on childhood and human development, but the same has not been done for the human being's acquisition of money. There are many books on money and personal finance, but most of them are not based on science, they are mostly based on the experience of the individuals writing the books, observations and a lot of trial and error. It is possible that given money is such a complex and hard to define subject, the only way to deal with it is by referring to real life examples, and not to theories or experiments carried out in a lab, because we all know that life is more complex than a lab.

We all become concerned when a child is not sitting, standing, walking or speaking past a certain age. We use statements like: "He is late!" As if we have some manual that defines when exactly children must sit. We actively potty train our children because we understand that past a certain age, it is no longer cute to change diapers. This is so abnormal that it is uncommon to find diapers for a six-year-old in the shops! We remain vigilant and committed with our potty training; we don't give up because it is hard, until the children reach a certain level of competence that will carry them through to adulthood and for the rest of their lives. No one is checking if their sixteen-year-old daughter knows how to go to the bathroom; you have trained her and you just know that she can.

For us to raise a generation that will handle money well, we need the same discipline and commitment when it comes to our own money. We also have a responsibility to help those under our care with their money.

Who is teaching you about money?

Our financial education must not be voluntary because money is just too important, and none of us can afford to go through life as if the money course is an elective. Most of us are adults now and we have not received any financial education and we wonder why our finances are the way they are! We must actively learn about money and each of us must be lifetime students of our personal finances. We must learn the principles of money and not just how to spend it. The commentaries given through television and the news give us the impression that money is to be chased daily, but the reality is that money takes more patience than it does speed. We must have a healthy relationship with money and not only reduce the description of our financial situations to extremes like poverty and wealth alone. We must appreciate money for the things that it can and cannot do. If we get all these and more right, then the greed, exploitation, bitterness, scarcity mentality, and wars around money may just end in our lifetime. Give yourself time to study how businesses track their financial status through their financial statements, so that you can have an idea of how to track the progress in your own life. Much study through accounting has been devoted to this science; therefore, there is no need for you to reinvent the wheel on this one.

The different ways to make money

In order to make money, you need to know that there are different ways to make money. There are options as to how you can accumulate wealth. In order to choose the option that is most suitable to you, it is your responsibility to conduct your own research.

In a world where information is readily available and accessible, most of us would get the moneymaking ideas we need at the click of a button.

In the following chapters, we will look at the different streams of income, which are the different ways to make money. As we explore each of the streams, I invite you to dig deeper so that you can:

- Maximise your current income stream/s.
- If you currently do not have any income, find the one that you can start with immediately.
- Focus on being good at one stream so that you don't confuse yourself with your fingers in too many pies at once.
- Don't be too quick to move to an income stream that is working for another person without doing a bit of homework.
- Believe in your capabilities. Don't walk into anything thinking you will fail. Start with a winning mind-set and work hard to realise your beliefs.

8. Get out of DEBT

Getting out of debt is a key part of your strategy to keep your money. Every person needs a budget and at a minimum, all of us must have a budget to give us a picture of what is happening in our finances every single month. Some of us know very well that a budget can also be a tool of discouragement. When you complete a budget and it shows you how indebted you are, the results can be utter hopelessness and despair. A budget is a planning tool but it is also a mirror, it is a reflection of what is happening in your finances. When you have too much debt and many repayments, it will be very hard to keep your money. In order to keep more of your money, you need to do two things: make more money and reduce your monthly commitments. If you have debt, you must include reducing or totally eliminating it, as part of your strategy to keep more of your money.

My personal encounter with debt

I had to learn very quickly to manage my bills and debt without worry; otherwise, I would have lost my mind. I was in debt before I even completed my engineering degree. By the time I started working, I had an overdraft and a credit card from the private bank, and I had a number of clothing accounts. As soon as I started working, I immediately bought a car I couldn't afford and I had to buy furniture, upgrade my wardrobe, drive all over the continent, and my meagre salary could not keep up with my demands. In no time, I had built-up a high credit card and overdraft balance and I had a number of them in different banks. I also had a couple of clothing accounts and loans to complete the picture.

By the time I realised that I was in debt, I decided that it was better to focus on increasing my income rather than focusing on reducing my spending and my debt. I had read books convincing me that only the uncreative person focuses on reducing costs, but the creative person focuses on making money through passive income. In the spirit of my newly found revelation, I joined network-marketing companies: one selling insurance and another selling products and services. I also started attending investment seminars and immediately started buying rental property and shares.

The more I read, the more optimistic I got. After reading Kim Kiyosaki's *Rich Woman*, I went on to buy 7 properties in a space of 2 years. It was all so exciting. I was under 30 and I felt like the world was my oyster. I just had to keep repeating this formula and if I continued on my buying streak, I would own at least 35 properties before I turned 40. The future looked bright. I was a landlord and I immediately forgot about my debts because I had something bigger to concentrate on.

During those days, it was so easy to get credit. I still can't believe that it was real. All you had to do was walk into the bank with your payslip and they didn't even bother to look at what else you owed. The bank made their assessment based on your payslip and the few accounts you had with them, they didn't consider accounts held with other banks. It was surreal! I had 5 home loans under my name and when I could no longer get the home loans approved under my name, I registered a company where I was the sole owner and continued on my buying spree.

Out of the blue, the house of cards came tumbling down. Everything that could go wrong started going wrong. First, the developers who were very greedy and highly leveraged started having problems completing new developments and they had to abandon certain projects, or buyers ended up receiving less features than what they paid for. Interest rates started going up every single month and the cost of servicing home loans increased exponentially. I had bought all my properties as new developments; offices that were converted to flats in an area in Johannesburg that was being revived. Property levies skyrocketed and the municipality introduced property rates. All these changes were designed to squeeze the money out of my rental business and the formula just didn't add up.

Profit = Rental income − (Homeloan repayments + rates + levies)

Everything was going up except my rental income and profit. Actually, I was making losses and the equations began to morph in a very unwholesome way into something like:

Loss = Rental income −

(repayments + rates + levies +

late payment costs + legal fees)

and even worse, I hadn't prepared myself for zero occupation where there was no rental income and the equation just became a horror movie:

Loss = Zero − (repayments + rates + levies +

late payment costs + legal fees)

Take this formula and multiply it by seven and you can start to have an idea of how much trouble I was in. At that time, I was working as a management consultant and the subsidy I had to pay on all those houses was more than half of my salary. My salary was not enough for me to live on as it was, and I had this extra money to put towards the houses. Somehow, I managed to keep making payments, they were late, the bank kept threatening me, lawyers kept sending me letters and I had many troublesome tenants. To make matters worse, my salary was at some kind of standstill or maybe I was just expecting it to perform miracles.

The turning point

The turning point came on one random payday when I went to withdraw money from the ATM. I went to the ATM to withdraw money before all the debit orders went off. At that time, I was making around R29 000 per month and my monthly obligations were more than R40 000. With a shortfall of R11 000, I had to make sure I took money out before there was nothing left. As I tried to withdraw, my card was retained by the machine and I went inside the branch to enquire.

"Your account is closed, Miss Pheeha."

"Why?"

"Your debit orders bounce every single month; we sent you a letter two months ago." I went quiet.

There's no way I would have received the letter because I hadn't paid the annual R350 renewal fee for the post box.

I was directed upstairs to go and speak to the consultant, who took me through a process of reducing my bond repayments. I was over-indebted. I was a professional, an engineer, a management consultant, and even a pastor, but my finances were in such a mess that I couldn't even buy myself a dress.

All my accounts were behind: the car, the houses, rates, levies, loans, credit cards, and overdrafts. I had to choose which accounts to pay because I could never afford to pay all of them in one month. My unsecured debt (that is everything excluding houses and cars) was in excess of R200 000 and I had no savings whatsoever.

I felt so much humiliation on that day. The failure to manage my finances had reduced me to this. My account was closed and I couldn't even access my salary for ten days because the money had already been returned to my employer. I felt like a failure, a thief, an irresponsible person, and on that day I decided I would change the way I handle my money.

How I got out of debt

I prayed for a miracle. I found verses in the bible on faith:

"Faith is the substance of things hoped for, the evidence of things not seen."

"The just shall live by faith."

"Have faith in God. If you say to this mountain be removed and be thrown into the sea…"

"We walk by faith and not by sight."

I found books that talked about money and devoured them. I stopped spending and made a plan to increase my income and eliminate debt. I sold 5 of the 7 properties to our investment club. I paid all overdue accounts and in two years, I had paid all of them off, including the car. It was two hard years of zero luxuries and determination to face my debts and restore my dignity.

The process was long and painful. Some things society just expects, like going out for dinner and being able to pay a mere R200, contributing for parties and events, travelling to weddings and funerals, bringing gifts to functions, buying clothes for preaching, having more than two pairs of shoes, buying underwear and toiletries. Everyone just expects you to be able to do that stuff, especially because at that time it appeared that everyone around me was managing, except me.

God was good and it all worked out, mainly because of the friends and family I have, and the determination and faith I got from all those scriptures. You may be in a similar situation or worse and I want to assure you that it is possible to get out of debt, no matter how deep in debt you are.

Get your head out of the sand

When most people are in debt, they experience a feeling similar to that of drowning, which is where the expression drowning in debt originated. When you have too much debt and you can't cope, you feel like you are suffocating and you can't breathe. The frustration of the debt could either lead to the over-indebted person choosing to ignore the debt just so that he can continue living his life or the other option is to be so depressed that the debt paralyses you and you just can't see a way out.

If you find yourself in debt, just take a step back, pause and simply calculate how much debt you have. Your ignorance about debt and your acts of wishing away the debt will not make it disappear, so do yourself a favour and calculate just how bad it is. Once you have determined the extent of your debt problem, choose a system that you can follow and apply it to your finances to eliminate the debt. Most of us are familiar with this question: "How do you eat an elephant?" And the answer is: "One bite at a time." When you know how much and whom you owe then you start attacking those debts one at a time. You apply discipline and creativity and in no time, you would have completed your task.

Follow a system to get out of debt

Let me remind you that personal finance is 80% behaviour and 20% knowledge, making it important to have a system to follow so that it can automate your behaviour. Most experts on finances agree on a snowball or waterfall approach to eliminating your debt. The different authors may have different variations of the approach, but the main principles are mentioned below:

1. Stop accumulating additional debt.
2. Make a list of all your debts, ranking them from lowest to highest 'remaining balance' (here authors will differ by ranking according to remaining balance, number of months left to pay off the debt, interest rate, etc.)

3. Next to each item listed make 3 columns:

Debt	Remaining Balance	Monthly Payment
Debt 1	R…	Payment 1 =Min p/m 1 +Any extra cash
Debt 2	R…	Payment 2
Debt 3	R…	Payment 3
Debt 4	R…	Payment 4
Debt 5	R…	Payment 5

4. Find any additional money in your budget (no matter how small);
5. Pay the minimum amount on every debt you have listed EXCEPT for the one you've marked with a "1";
6. On this first debt to be paid off, pay the minimum amount due plus all the additional money you could find from your budget;
7. Keep doing this each month until your first debt is paid off, and then scratch that first debt off your list.
8. Pay the minimum amount due on every debt you have EXCEPT for the one you've marked with a "2". To this debt pay the minimum amount due, PLUS the entire amount you've been paying on debt 1.

Debt	Remaining Balance	Monthly Payment
Debt 2	R…	Payment (1+2)

Debt 3	R...	Payment 3
Debt 4	R...	Payment 4
Debt 5	R...	Payment 5

and....

Debt	Remaining Balance	Monthly Payment
Debt 3	R...	Payment (1+2+3)
Debt 4	R...	Payment 4
Debt 5	R...	Payment 5

and continue until all debts are paid off...

This compounding (Payment 1+2+3, etc.) approach of payments is the reason why this system is called a debt snowball or waterfall, because as you go down on the list, the monthly payments keep increasing just like a snowball or a waterfall under gravity.

Applying the formula to your debt

The power of this information is in the fact that you must apply it, immediately, now. Take a short break from reading the book and put a bit of work on your finances.

Find a piece of paper (preferably a book that you will not easily throw away) or an electronic device (smartphone, laptop, tablet, etc.) and write down every single debt you have. Rank your debt according to the system we described earlier and try your best not to worry about the total.

Now ask yourself: "Where can I get additional money to put towards eliminating my debt?" Would you be able to; sell some things for a profit, sell things you don't need anymore, get paid overtime at work, take on an extra job, give up on some luxuries like expensive nail and hair treatments, eating out less, putting a temporary pause on clothes shopping, etc.?

You need to be creative to find ways to make an additional income. I have friends who drive family cars at funerals during weekends, place domestic workers for a fee, use a carpool with friends to reduce fuel costs, find a roommate, enter a seasonal business like selling ice or fireworks during the festive season, etc. Look beyond your comfort zone and find new ways to bring more money to help with your debt. Be disciplined in paying off that debt; that is all it takes.

9. Understand income streams

There are many ways to make money, and when you consider all the options it becomes easy to identify one that is most suitable to your skills, personality, interests and passions. This book will not exhaust all the streams of income but for most of us, knowing that there are different ways to earn money is so liberating. This section of the book is meant to entice you into discovering the streams of income that are available out there. It deals with the first part of the principle we are teaching here; make money.

A perfect income stream is one that allows you to use your natural talents while you make money but any stream that will make money in a legal and moral manner is just as good. In the pursuit of the perfect income stream, most people wait for their passions to produce an income. There's a famous picture of a female skeleton sitting on a park bench with the caption: "waiting for the perfect man." The picture tells it all, we all strive for perfection but often we need to engage in "good enough" and through our effort and commitment, good enough will become perfect. Some people are fortunate in that they immediately merge their passions and income generating activities, but most people will only reach that sweet spot later in life.

I am currently involved in the kind of work that I know I am called for and in a small way, it is starting to make money, but that is not where I started. Often the people who are making money from their passion tend to make the rest of us who are still slaving in our jobs or businesses feel bad. Some of us who are working in areas different from our passion are at times filled with guilt and shame, as if we are betraying our true self. Life is a journey and part of that journey involves finding that sweet spot where your talents merge with income generation. If you have arrived at that sweet spot, don't look down on those of us who are still searching.

"Find your passion and you never have to work another day in your life!" they say, and "Do what you love and you never have to work another day in your life." In reality, for most people, our love and our passion don't generate enough money to even pay the basic bills. When your passion falls short of what you need to provide for your lifestyle, then you need to consider other streams of income. If you are fortunate, one of those streams or even all could be the passion stream. The job you hate that pays the bills may not be so unbearable if you are working on your passion somewhere else.

Music may be your passion but you may not be talented enough to be paid for your music, so you could opt to keep your job as an engineer and sing in the church choir without being paid. A lot of frustration can come upon the musician who decides to only be involved in music because he doesn't want to wander far away from his passion. Passion doesn't always pay the bills but money does.

The salary

Most of us understand how a salary works. It is predictable; it comes at an agreed date. It is not completely dependent on personal effort and it grows with a steady rate that we can justify with concepts like inflation, cost of living adjustment, etc. Because we understand this form of income very well, we spend most of our lives desiring it, we pursue it with everything we have and when we can't find it, we live in despair and frustration. The person who has never worked in his or her life is on the verge of hopelessness because a job would answer all the problems they experience. The fired and retrenched person is desperately looking for their next assignment because they cannot imagine how they would live without the much-needed salary.

In a world where jobs are few and good jobs are even fewer, we need to learn about other sources of income. A job is simply a means to trade your time for money. In order for a person to be gainfully employed, it means that someone considered their time (and the value that time brings to an enterprise) and put a price on it (the salary that the enterprise is willing to pay the employee). In a traditional sense, we are socialised to give our time to one enterprise and then receive a salary at a set date. One can choose to give their time to one enterprise or they can choose to give their time to different enterprises or individuals and instead of being paid by one organisation, they would then receive payment from all the persons that are benefiting from their time and value.

You don't have to limit yourself to one stream of income

In our country, there is a common practise where maids would work for different households. The maid would work for one day a week at 7 different houses and be paid by each household. In most cases, each household cannot afford to pay a maid to come 7 days a week, and if the maid only worked for one household, she would not make enough money to live on. This is the concept of multiple streams of income. In this example, the nature of the maid's streams of income is the same, but they don't have to be.

When I was a student, I used to tutor the university students in Maths, high school learners in Maths and Science in the township, and ran a tuck shop in one of the residences on campus. The streams looked insignificant when considered individually, but together they added up. The more you learn about each stream of income, the more you can optimise it. It's easier to understand the game when you are playing, rather than when you advise from the side-lines.

My sister runs a pre-school, sows and sells cartoon character bedding for the kids, runs a holiday programme at her school, provides scholar transport, and she places maids for a fee. These are all different streams of income, but they revolve around her one passion: children.

Then there is my uncle who has a job as an executive. He buys property and rents it out, he sells property for capital gain, and he buys shares in businesses.

Let me end with my mom who ran a canteen in one of the government departments during weekdays, ran a chill-out spot during the weekends and holidays, and still managed to sell pickled mangoes, biscuits, clothes, some she made and some she was reselling and the list goes on and on.

We appreciate and celebrate big conglomerates when they have multiple income streams. We know that it is a secret to their success but when we have to apply the same secret in our own lives, it appears to be too exhausting.

One of the main reasons why unemployed people don't want to hear the advice that they should start a business instead of looking for a job, is because we somehow make them believe that they can only choose one option. When a person is desperately looking for a job we work so hard convincing them not to look for a job, but instead to start a business or at the very least to start selling something. The real advice we need to give job seekers is that while they wait for their job to manifest, they could use the additional time they have to start an additional stream of income, which may continue even after they have found a job.

10. Find a Job[5]

Oh how I wish I had appreciated my job when I had it, but it is gone now, never to come again. When I knew that my former boss was going to fire me, I didn't even lift my finger to try to save my job. As soon as I was fired, I simply left. Throughout the hearing I knew that I was going to be fired, I never even made a single prayer asking God to save the job. I didn't attempt to save the job because deep down I always believed that I could do better. Knowing deep in my heart that I could do better contributed to how I felt about the job; I despised my job and there was no way I could fight for a job that was beneath me. If only I had understood that the job doesn't define me, it was simply a part of the multiple income streams that I could have in my life, I would have had a different view. If I had my job right now, my bank account would be telling a very different story. Currently, my bank account is speaking of neglect, negative balances, dishonoured payments and a drought of deposits.

I have always loved George S. Clason's classic, *The richest man in Babylon*. I have read the book more times than I care to remember; truth is I'm too embarrassed to mention the number of times I have read it. Even when I was employed, I would take time aside and devour the book as if I'm hearing the parables for the first time in my

---

[5] Chapter discusses lessons from George S. Clason's: The Richest Man in Babylon

life. Now that I have no work, the words from the book are even more powerful, especially as they relate to work. Let me take a few minutes and tell you about the exploits of a slave turned billionaire called Sharru Nada.

The benefits of a job

Sharru Nada was sold into slavery by his family because he was placed as security for a crime that his brother committed. When he was on his journey to be sold into slavery in Babylon, he met a fellow slave called Megiddo who taught him a few principles about work:

- Make work your best friend and it will give you everything you desire.
- Don't worry about the fact that your work is unrecognised; work will always make you a better person.
- Work will help you recover from trouble and misfortune.
- Work can help you buy your freedom (In Sharru's days, it was freedom from slavery but in our day, we have slavery of another kind. Those who know it call it financial freedom: not having to work another day in your life but choosing to work. When you don't have financial freedom, you remain a slave).
- Decide what you desire, and work will help you achieve it.
- Work will become your best helper, enabling you to recapture your confidence and your skills.

- When you have nothing, work is your only way to make money, therefore, do yourself a favour and enjoy working regardless of the type of work you find.
- There will always be a generous reward for every effort you make at work.
- All laziness and half-hearted efforts will catch up with you at some point.
- Work will rescue you in the time of your greatest distress.

Find any job

At the end of their slave voyage, Sharru Nada and his fellow slaves were taken to the slave market where potential slave owners were looking to buy slaves. When they got there, many of the other slaves pulled back and were not comfortable with being put up for sale, but both Megiddo and Sharru spoke to all the potential buyers and displayed their skills with enthusiasm. At the end, Megiddo was bought by a farmer and Sharru was bought by a baker. This tale is so extreme in that it speaks of the sale of human beings, which is now illegal, but if you look beyond the slavery, you will see that it speaks of today's corporate world where all of us are competing to sell our skills.

In school, there is no emphasis on entering the corporate world and selling our skills and ourselves. Sharru was hired by a baker because he demonstrated enthusiasm and a willingness to learn, he didn't know anything about baking. Every year school leavers and graduates, retrenched and fired people join the job market. Most of them could learn from the enthusiasm of Sharru and Megiddo in displaying their skills, attitude and aptitude. In a world where employers are inundated with a sea of résumés, what sets you apart? How willing are you to stand out from the crowd and approach a potential employer? How willing are you to start a job you don't know, or a job that you feel is beneath your qualifications? If a man was willing to sell himself for a job he wouldn't even be paid for as a slave, are we really doing enough to enter the corporate world?

Over deliver in every job

Your willingness, attitude, how well you answer interview questions, how you look, maybe even your academic transcript will get you the job, but what really matters is what you do when you get to that job. When Sharru Nada arrived at his new job, he learnt everything about baking and he got so good that the baker had nothing to do. You must be so good that you replace your boss's job even without occupying his position. Sharru came up with new ideas, and he found creative ways to implement them. In our society today, there is no shortage of good ideas but what we are looking for is the employee who will not only introduce his ideas, but who will also fold his sleeves and go into the trenches.

Companies are filled with people who know how things can be done better, but those same people tell themselves that the company is not worth their ideas for many reasons. Maybe they are bitter because they earn too little, or they feel undermined or they have decided that they will only contribute intellectually after they have received recognition. You aren't recognised by hogging your ideas, you can only be recognised for the ideas you contribute and help implement. Others have decided that they will reserve their best ideas for a time when they run their own companies. They don't realise that ideas are not finite, the more you use ideas, the easier they are to generate. That is why creative people who work in jobs where they constantly brainstorm ideas seem to have a sea of ideas.

Creativity follows the Matthew rule: "For whoever has, to him more will be given, and he will have abundance; but whoever does not have, even what he has will be taken away from him." So harsh, yet so true. The more ideas you generate and contribute, the more ideas you will have and if you have few and don't use the few you have, the next thing you know you just cannot think of a single idea. Sounds familiar? Contribute the single idea you have and watch it grow into a stream of fresh ideas.

Sharru did his work well but he also helped the maid. You need to understand that you are not in the corporate world for selfish ambition only, look for opportunities to add value to others and to make yourself a valuable member of every team that you are a part of.

Sharru was so good at his work, he finished early and he started looking for more opportunities to be of greater use to his master. He came up with a new income stream; he made more cakes that they could sell in the streets. As a slave, he negotiated to keep half of the money after they had paid all the costs. He made a tray and wore one of his master's old clothes and with enthusiasm he went to the streets to sell the cakes. The same maid that Sharru helped to carry heavy things around the house, patched the old suit for Sharru to get him ready to start selling cakes.

When we go out of our way to help people in the workplace, we are not doing so with the hope that they will also help us, but it is inevitable, as we help others they will always be on the lookout for opportunities to help us when we need it.

Intrapreneurship

Intrapreneurship is defined as starting a business within an existing business. You don't go out on your own but you use the company's resources to start a new business for the company. If you are fortunate, as in the case of Sharru, you can negotiate a share of the sales from the new business instead of an increase in salary.

On the first day of selling, Sharru had a slow start. In the morning, people were not hungry, but as lunch approached and people became hungry they bought all his cakes. Sharru continued and soon he understood the trends of his business. People bought during lunch mostly and in no time he had regular customers, he knew where to go. The thing with understanding an industry, or business or a product, is that it takes more than reading a book, watching the news, conducting market research or writing a business plan. We understand stuff by doing and the more you get involved in your work, the more understanding and wisdom and ultimately, luck you will attract.

A job will bring you closer to your purpose

As Sharru continued to work, he figured out what he wanted to do with his life. During his time working for the baker, he discovered that he was good at selling things and he decided to become a merchant, that was his dream and he discovered it whilst working as a slave. You may not be in your dream job, but your current job will help you discover what your dream job is. Baking introduced Sharru to his ultimate purpose of being a merchant. Sharru would never have known that he wants to be a merchant if he hadn't started selling the baked goods on his own, he would also never have learnt just how good he was at it.

Our society has spoken so negatively about jobs with things like: "If you are not working on your dream, someone else will pay you to work on theirs." We make statements like these as if they are bad but in fact, many of us will discover what our dream is by working on someone else's dream. Most people define financial freedom as stopping to work as if working is a bad thing. These concepts have made most of us to hate and resent work instead of making it our best friend.

Work is not your enemy, don't hate it! You will never give yourself to something that you hate. Bishop Tudor Bismark once preached and made this example: He asked his driver to come up to the stage and play the piano, the driver played and it was horrible. He then asked the piano player, who happened to be one of the best in the country, to play and he played a magical melody. The bishop then went on to explain that the difference between the driver and the piano player was that the piano player had given himself to the piano. He had given himself to the piano and when he wanted music from the piano, the piano kindly obliged and gave of itself to him.

Work gives you the opportunity to truly give yourself to something. A routine comes with work: arriving at a certain time, punctuality, professionalism, meetings, teamwork, managing upwards and downwards, following rules, managing your career, following instructions, giving instructions, etc. The benefits of work are endless, you give yourself to the job and it gives you back so much more. You enter a job as a young unpolished girl or boy and you come out from the other side as a polished professional with skills and experience you never imagined you could possess. You now know how to write reports, run meetings, make financial projections, write proposals and so much more.

Challenges at work

Sharru Nada was climbing the corporate ladder, and well on his way to buying his freedom. He had calculated how much it would take him to buy back his ownership from his master and he had calculated how much time it would take him to save that money. What happened next was unexpected and unfortunate.

Sharru's master had nothing to do because of Sharru's excellent work. He was idle and ended up gambling. In order to pay his gambling debts, he used Sharru Nada's title as security. One day the person that his master owed came to collect Sharru. In a moment, Sharru Nada moved from being in a good environment where he was growing, to working in a horrible environment that almost killed him.

When Sharru arrived at his new job, he demonstrated the same enthusiasm and willingness to work. This time he even had experience and a track record to indicate what a good slave he had been. Not only was the work and the environment horrible, but his boss and the owner of the company hated the job. The work was too big and the company was under a lot of pressure to finish the project with insufficient resources. At first, Sharru worked with good will, but as the months continued, his spirit began to break and he became sick. He could no longer sleep or even eat and he gave up all hope. He stopped believing in the principle of working because he realised that work did not bring him joy and success.

Sharru had a lot of questions and no answers. Why is it that life singled some people out and rewarded them for their hard work, while he seemed to be constantly pursued by bad luck? Why did the indiscretion of others land him in slavery every time? Is he cursed? Are there some people who are not meant to succeed? In his state of confusion, someone who had admired his hard work when he still sold the cakes paid his ransom and freed him from slavery. The person who paid for Sharru's freedom was a person he had helped in the marketplace. He was only sharing with him the importance of hard work, but what he didn't know was that his words made a big impact on his saviour. God will never allow your efforts to go unrewarded and no matter how dark things look, He will make a way.

Sharru Nada went on to be a successful merchant, applying all the work principles he had learnt from Megiddo to build his business empire. His first partner was the same man who had paid for his freedom. This man looked for him because he had witnessed first-hand Sharru's relationship with work. He knew for sure that his business would succeed with a partner like him.

This story is so dramatic, but it is no different from the everyday life of the employee. For many people, just when they were steadily rising through the ranks, something happens and snatches everything away. You could be falsely accused, be placed in a very difficult project where you are just not coping, not get along with your boss or your team, make a costly mistake that gets you fired, or find yourself in any other situation that could lead either to you losing your job or to the workplace becoming a very hostile environment. You could be retrenched, or your contract may end or you may be fired or even be forced into resigning. Nothing in the workplace is guaranteed and your approach to work must not only apply when the environment is right. The successful employee must be able to navigate not only the healthy work environment but also the hostile and toxic environment. Employees find themselves in a myriad of dynamics in the different work environments: the big corporate, the government institution, the NGO, the family business, the small enterprise, the one man show, etc. Your success is not only in how well you execute your duties, but also in managing the environment that you find yourself in.

Understand the environment you work in

When I started out as a management consultant, I never understood what the partners were on about when they kept saying I must demonstrate my value proposition! In my world, my work should speak for itself and the fact that I made it through the interview process was enough demonstration of value proposition. No one had taught me the concept of selling myself to management and demonstrating my capabilities and deliverables. To me it all seemed like bragging and sucking up, and I was raised to be a humble hard working woman who delivered quietly and consistently. I was then surprised when colleagues who were less talented and who didn't work as hard were promoted and always preferred on project teams. I quickly had to learn that delivery is only one aspect of the skills required in the workplace; there are other skills, which are just as important. In a company where we sold our services, demonstrating your individual value proposition was just as important as delivery, and neglecting it was the difference between a bonus and being performance managed out of the firm.

When I changed careers to government, I then realised that building relationships was the most important skill I needed. Lobbying is not only something that you need to win elections in a political party, but you lobby to get your proposals approved and to ensure that discussions around your presentations are not hostile. It didn't matter how pretty and informative my slides were, if the influential people were not lobbied prior to the cabinet meetings, I was going to be slaughtered.

My experience working for a family business that was led by a husband and wife team was the opposite of the government institution I worked in. In the family business, you should not be seen to have lobbied one partner and not the other. Presentations would quickly deteriorate to family fights and if you did not play your cards right, you could be left alone with the screen and chair as your audience. In a family business you need to understand that there is no objectivity, there are two people that own this thing and your role is to work according to their wishes and often times, there is nowhere to escalate your issues to.

There is a wide variety of workplaces and what each employee needs to figure out is simply this: what does it take to go to the top, to earn more, to secure this particular stream of income? Most people will always make more than 75% of their income from a job, don't treat it casually, it is your livelihood and it is honourable to work.

11. Start a Business

All workplaces were once a business that someone or some people started. The businesses we start today are the jobs of tomorrow. For many average people though, we find that starting a business is so different from getting a job. With a job, as soon as you accept your offer of employment, you are guaranteed that on the agreed date your money will be paid into your account. A business is a totally different animal. It may look profitable on paper and the concept may be solid and well thought through, but for as long as no one is buying you can count the money on paper and if it is not in your bank account, you are left struggling and desperate.

There are many statistics around the failure of businesses, as well as the reasons for that failure, but I will not get into that debate. The purpose of this chapter is to give you a few real examples about ordinary business people, so that most of us can stop romanticising owning a business and get on with the hard work and fun of setting up and running successful businesses.

Our approach to business in this book is to encourage you to set up a business as an additional stream of income. The idea is not to write an exhaustive book on business, but to demonstrate to you that each of us has the capacity to set up something as early as we possibly can in life. If it is correctly set up, a business can take care of you with minimal requirement on your time. A good business will also give you the opportunity to leverage other people's time, resources, skills and money to fulfil both your dream and theirs. Some people may be lucky and their business can go on to become wildly successful and well known, but that should never take away from the businessperson who sustainably runs a profitable business. Running one taxi that makes R20 000 per month may not seem glamorous, but if you add it to all the other income in your life, you will realise that it may be worthwhile to get involved. A small café or a franchise may look insignificant when you consider it in isolation, but it could be the breakthrough you are looking for if it brings an additional fifty grand into your existing endeavours.

Here we are making a case for a well thought out side business, and not necessarily speaking to the all-out entrepreneur that feels called. I learnt early from my parents about getting side businesses to pay for recurring expenses in our home. My mother set up a garden and sold vegetables that in turn paid for the helper, the gardener and maintenance in the house. Instead of getting daily pocket money as a young girl, I used to sell popcorn during the holidays to fund my financial needs when schools opened. Our house was always selling something so that we never had to ask my mom for money to buy bread or anything else that was finished in the house. At any given time, the child who was home was responsible for the business; from replenishing stock to making sure that the business remained profitable. I suspect that this may be the reason why all my siblings are running their own businesses.

Starting a business takes patience

My sister is very passionate about kids, and for as long as I can remember, she always wanted to open a school. She studied at the most reputable school in the continent and completed her diploma. She completed her practical work at a well-run school, prepared a business plan, attended a business incubator with a coach, and the works. She converted a residential property into a school as per the business plan, hired staff, hit the streets with marketing and all she needed was a mere thirty children for the school to break even and pay her a reasonable salary. Month after month, she waited for her thirty children to come and only after two years does it appear that she will finally get the thirty children.

A business doesn't operate like a clock. Just when you think you are reaching your targeted number of children, some families move out of town and therefore take their children with them. On paper it all makes sense. If it were an exam, she would get full marks or if it were a report she had to submit to her boss, she would be rated as an overachiever at work. In business though, things are very different… we measure you by your profits and cash flow.

This lag, false start or delay is the one thing that discourages most business people and they end up closing shop before time. My sister has been at it for two years and finally her school is profitable. The beginning of a business needs patience and flexibility. In some cases, you just have to wait it out and keep doing what you are doing and in other cases, you have to be flexible enough to change your plans mid-air. As you set up this income stream for yourself, remember that a business has a very unpredictable lifestyle. The person running the business is more important than the actual business and you need to prepare yourself to work on the business until it produces the income you are looking for.

Running a business requires flexibility

My dad had been running his pest control business for more than ten years when things suddenly changed in his environment. He had been the only black supplier of pest control services to government in his province when other players surfaced. The priorities of government changed, there was an emphasis on empowering young people and women and a move away from long-term contracts. My dad was forced to reprioritise and focus more on getting private clients. He could have written an article or an academic paper on the impact of policy changes on small businesses, but that wouldn't change his bottom-line.

Sometimes when direction changes in your field, you are forced to acquire new skills and expertise. My dad moved from completing tender documents for government to writing unsolicited proposals for the private sector. It required not only different skills, but also a different mind-set. Most businesses die at the point of transition. You have to be flexible enough to 'change with the times' because that is what is required to take your business to the next level. If you manage to take your business to the next level, you will also command higher income from it. The idea is not only to have multiple streams of income, but also to optimise and maximise each of the streams.

A successful business owner understands cash flow

When I started writing, I did the maths and focused on the projections, but I was not prepared for the boxes of books that would take an entire year to sell. I hadn't prepared for the commutes to different places just so I can get my books in front of audiences that sometimes didn't even buy. I would speak to crowds who would give me a standing ovation, and then only purchase 3 books. No one had prepared me for just how painful the journey would be. On paper, my strategies made lots of sense but somehow the execution wasn't quite what I had anticipated.

I believe in research, business plans and projections, but at this point I must emphasise that nothing, absolutely nothing, can replace running the business and learning from experience. At some point, you have to close your notepad and get into running a business. There's also a fear around starting a business that can only be overcome by the person who starts.

The rationale I used when deciding about my books business was very simple. Since I was already travelling extensively preaching and speaking to different audiences, people were always asking for material that I could leave behind. I had quite a lot of material from preparation notes and a book was a natural next step. I consolidated my notes and got a book self-published after many sleepless nights. I realised that the more copies you printed, then the lower your printing costs became. So it made perfect sense that I start with a 'conservative' 2 000 copies.

I just completed a back of the napkin calculation about what the profit would be, but I hadn't calculated how much time I would need to sell 2 000 books. I had extrapolated the enquiries of one or two people at an event to conclude that everyone in the audience would be falling over themselves to buy my books. I never imagined that my living room would become a warehouse for books and that my car would be turned into a delivery vehicle.

If you are starting a business, be determined to be a fast learner. Don't make the same mistake twice in business and don't bring your ego into your business. Be quick to identify and rectify your mistakes, so that they don't kill the business. I was very slow to change, I printed three more batches of 2 000 but the last two I printed were 300 and 500 respectively. I learnt slowly and my living room can testify, and I do hope that in your own business you react much faster than I did.

I don't want to bore you with tales of all the times when I was broke, but had at least half a million worth of stock in my house. As you create business as an additional stream of income, set it up in such a way that it doesn't cripple all the other streams. Don't take every single cent from your job and tie it up in your business to the point that you can't even afford a slice of bread. Pace yourself as you set up the business and appreciate the slow start, because when the business builds momentum, you will have to do very little to keep it going.

The owner must continue even after the business has failed

I remember a long time ago, three friends and I had this brilliant idea to go to Durban and start a photography business to make some money over the Christmas holidays. You need to understand, this was during a time when digital photography and instant printing was pure innovation, let alone putting any kind of text on the photo. We purchased a digital camera, a printer, photo quality paper and got into my little 1.3 litre car, and drove 600 kilometres to the beach. When we arrived, the beach was full of excited holidaymakers, and trying to convince them to purchase our services was a walk in the park.

Families and couples on holiday couldn't get enough of our calendars with their photos by the beach; they had all sorts of portraits telling the story of their holiday. To them, this was the best memento they could ever bring from their holiday. Business was booming and we were already projecting just how rich we would be after one month. The demand was so high that we couldn't even keep up.

The one thing that our little photography empire was not ready for was the response from all the authorised photographers on the beach. We didn't even know that there were people that were licensed to take photos on the beach – talk about not doing your research, and they were bullies of note. Those photographers shut us down in a day because people didn't want their services anymore. We offered a superior product with additional services that they could not match. We found ourselves stuck with all the equipment and we couldn't even take a single photo for fear of being beaten up or even killed. (Okay, I added a little drama there!)

Business doesn't follow a script. You would hear people talking about how they started their business and they make it sound like they stumbled into it with very little effort. The irony though is that when you are trying everything to make your business work out, it just doesn't and you end up thinking that the stories you hear are fake. When I attend business seminars and I listen to other people's journeys and how scripted they all sound, I tend to think either I'm not cut out for this business thing or some of these people are omitting the real struggles that got them to the top.

It is important that you should never get attached to any kind of business. Businesses fail all the time, and even though it might hurt and feel personal, when your business fails, it is just one of many other businesses that have failed. The trick with business failure is that you must learn early enough to differentiate between yourself and the business. When the business fails, I hope you will have the guts to quickly fold it and move on to establishing another one. The challenge though is that when a business fails, most of us end up losing money. The failure of our photography business left me with unused cameras, printers and no enthusiasm to try again. This loss of money results in many business owners staying for longer than they should in a business, in an effort to recover their losses. Try to manage your risk in such a way that the failure of a business doesn't sink you financially. Always remember what your goal is with this business, simply creating an additional stream of income.

Don't give up

I know there seems to be more stories of business failure than business success. Some random security guard, after I told him that I own a business, started telling me his business story. He used to work for a company that manufactured cupboards and he was very good. One of the company's clients saw his good workmanship and work ethic and invited him and another employee to start a business and the client committed to support their new venture. The two of them resigned and started a business and the next thing he knows, his colleague ran away with the business and somehow removed his name from the business documents (I wonder if his name was ever there to start with). So when I met him, he was a security guard and he could only relate tales of how he almost made it in life.

I know of many relatives and friends who invested in catering equipment that is now gathering dust in their garages and occupying space that was meant for the car. Others have bought tents, chairs, and decorating items, which occasionally get used by relatives when they have parties. I don't have to go very far to see boxes of books behind my couch to see that most times the business you see on paper is not the business you experience in real life.

I know enough people who have registered businesses, opened bank accounts, and have never made a single cent. Some businesses have only existed to pay for bank account fees and nothing else. Yet, there are other people who got deals even before they had a registered business or bank account and they had to organise all their paperwork retrospectively. I always pray that I may be one of those people who just wakes up one day and a deal just miraculously lands on my lap.

This information is not to discourage you from starting a business; this is an attempt from my side to give you a reality check. This is to say to you, business is not like school or a job, so when you hit those speed humps on your business journey that is not the time to quit. In order to create or develop business as a stream of income you will need an extra dose of perseverance and flexibility.

In our village, when a family has enough money they dig a borehole so that they can have their own supply of water and not have to depend on the unreliable government supply. The thing with digging a borehole is that you don't know for sure at what level you will strike water and for as long as you haven't struck the water, you cannot give up. Approach your business like digging a well; don't give up until you have struck water and in this case, don't give up until you have a profitable and sustainable business. Don't forget our objective with this thing of starting a business… creating an additional stream of income.

12. Make Passive Income

We all want passive income and as soon as I have described it, you will realise that you also want it. Passive income is money that comes in whether you are sleeping, travelling or working. I tell anyone who would listen that I want a tollgate kind of business, no matter where you are, when a car passes your tollgate, the driver has to pay.

There is upfront planning required in setting up a tollgate kind of business and it needs people who have a long-term view and who are not afraid of making the upfront investment. Examples of passive income include, but are not limited to the following:

1) Property
2) Being a franchisor
3) Creating content (Books, Music, Movies, Courses, etc.)
4) Buying and selling shares
5) Commodities, shares and FOREX
6) Crypto currencies

Investment property

I read Robert Kiyosaki's *Rich Dad Poor Dad* and felt like a brand new world opened up before me. The book spoke mostly about the USA, but I firmly believed that the same principles could be applied right where I was in sunny South Africa. I kept reading about investing in real estate, residential rental property to be exact, and I made up my mind that it was my asset of choice.

I went on to attend seminars on the same subject and met with people that had made a success of investing in property. I was encouraged and all I needed was my first deal. I must confess right here at the very beginning, that even though I read the entire book, I neglected some of the most important considerations when investing in rental property. Rental yields, positive cash flow and total cost of ownership, where just inconveniences for me. All I wanted to know was is the property beautiful, can I raise the deposit and will the bank give me the money to buy it.

A friend who was also a business mentor at that time had a couple of bachelor units in a property that was located next to the university. The unit would cost me R165 000 and it had a value of no less than R250 000. I was excited, I approached the bank for a loan and in no time, I was the landlady that I had been dreaming and praying about.

I found two students who were tenants and all went well for the first couple of months, until they stopped taking my calls and paying rent. I went to the property to check and found it in a mess. After much back and forth and broken promises, I finally evicted them and my first lesson in property was officially in session. I had to personally clean that mess and since I couldn't get tenants and didn't have a place to stay, I decided to live there.

I ultimately sold the unit for R270 000 and made a profit. After my first taste of property success, I bought 7 additional property within a period of 18 months.

Be careful of partially applying a system that works

My method of buying rental property was simple. I would pay the required deposit, which was often much less than 1 per cent of the actual property cost and then apply for 100% finance from the bank. I bought properties that looked beautiful and modern, usually brand new developments with extra shiny things like appliances and modern finishes. All the properties were overpriced, but I was buying with my heart and never with my head. The properties were bought off-plan (which means before construction was complete) and payment was only due on completion.

The excitement of being an owner of 7 properties cannot be described in words but it was all short-lived when it appeared that everything that could go wrong was going wrong.

First, all the properties were ready at the same time.

Secondly, as soon as I was required to make repayments to the bank, interest rates started going up and my interest payments were increasing every three months.

Thirdly, the city started making changes and there were additional municipality rates that were required for all sectional title units.

Fourthly, the management companies just kept raising levies at every single general meeting and raising special levies at a whim.

Lastly, tenants were troublesome. They would be late with payments or not pay at all, or they would run away without paying rent.

Instead of bringing me wealth, my rental property was just a painful money-sucking parasite. Everything I had read told me that property appreciates in value but for some reason mine seemed to be depreciating.

Learn from your mistakes and make better decisions

Since those 7 acquisitions, I have made 3 more purchases but my method has changed. I bought two rental units cash and the properties are cash-flow positive. I bought another unit and put down a 40% deposit.

- ✓ Getting a 100% loan from the bank may be exciting but for most of us, it is just an indication that you don't afford the property.
- ✓ When creating a business case for each rental property, make sure the cash flow is positive. Don't buy rental property that requires you to take money from your personal accounts monthly to subsidise the rental monthly costs.

- ✓ Account for all costs involved. Don't just look at the bond repayments. On some of my properties, the levies and rate costs were equal to the bond repayments.
- ✓ Not all property purchases are wise, some purchases can bankrupt you and take money out of your pocket that you could be investing for a real return.
- ✓ There are such things as bad property purchases but there are also good ones.

I have 4 properties now that are just a dream. The tenants cover all the costs and there's still money left over. All the properties are cash flow positive and it comes down to how they are financed and managed. You can't out-manage a badly financed property. Rental property can be one of the easiest form of passive income when it is done right. All you have to do is pay the deposit, get finance and find a good tenant and the rest is history. The journey will just be one where you own a property but the tenant will pay for all the monthly costs and even put money in your pocket, even if that money is R1 it is still worth it.

I have sold two rental properties in my life and the sale has taught me just how amazing rental property that is bought right can be. Receiving profit from those two sales made me realise that rental property, if done right, can truly help many of us reach our dreams.

I recently visited a friend who lives in a mansion. When I asked her how she managed to buy such a lovely house she told me that she had been buying houses at auctions and selling them for a profit. That is how she made her money and that is why she lives in the lap of luxury.

It is important that you do your own research on the different passive income streams so that you can choose one or a couple and pursue them. Make passive income a part of your finance strategy. Find out why it may be worthwhile to franchise your business system instead of only thinking about buying a franchise. Don't be afraid of things like trading and crypto currency, instead research them and decide based on facts whether or not it is something you would want to pursue. Proverbs says: "My people perish because of lack of knowledge. Don't allow ignorance to be the reason why you perish financially."

13. Become part of Network Marketing

I have tried my hand on this stream of income and I came out with the decision that it is surely not for me. Sometimes when I listen to people who are wealthy because of this stream of income, I wonder if I gave up too easily, didn't have the right level of commitment or it was just bad luck. Whatever my reason for not succeeding, I could never conclude that network marketing does not work.

When you decide where to invest your time, you consider what, in project management and finance, we call a rate of return. In the interest of not getting too technical, a rate of return is defined simply as the gain or loss you get from your investment over a specified time-period. Most of us know how to consider our investment in terms of the money we put down, but so many of us do not know how to put a value to our time, energy and effort. While we calculate the amount of money we are making from network marketing efforts, we need to consider our time as well. Network marketers often invest all their time in building a business and it is important that they must build a real business.

Are you building a real business?

If you choose to make money through this stream of income here are a few things to consider:

- ✓ Build a business that can operate without you. Most network marketing businesses stop paying an income to the business owner as soon as the business owner stops working. In this case, the network marketer is not building a business but is simply earning a commission on selling products and on introducing other salespeople to the company.
- ✓ Look at the network marketing business model and ensure that there will be passive income.
- ✓ Ask the difficult questions; what will happen to my business when I die or am no longer able to run the business?
- ✓ Consider if the products are not in conflict with your values (it's very difficult to sell an overpriced insurance policy that you don't even believe in).
- ✓ There is a difference between a legitimate business where the profits that should have gone to the distribution network are now passed on to network marketers, and overpriced products that people only buy because they support you or because they are greedy to make money from suckers who can't tell the true value of the product. Such businesses will not be sustainable and as a network marketer, you will work very hard and end up having built nothing.

Advantages of network marketing

The most positive thing to consider in network marketing besides the obvious monetary reward is the educational programmes that all good network-marketing companies have. All good network marketing companies have a foundation of an educational programme that is meant to make the individual business owner a more confident person, up skilled with all the necessary qualities to run a business successfully. There are very few programmes with the consistency of a network marketing company to assist the individual with self-actualisation and with the tools needed to be an entrepreneur.

Another advantage of being part of a network marketing company is; surrounding yourself with like-minded people who will support and encourage you on your journey. Entrepreneurship can be a very lonely path and joining a network marketing company might just provide the push some of us need to persevere in business.

The last thing and maybe the most important, is all those electrifying events that network marketers organise on a regular basis. Those events can be as powerful as a charismatic church service, you come out of there feeling like you can conquer the world. For many of us, our worlds are full of so much adversity that a few hours or days to focus on your potential and to celebrate the success of others is just what we need to inject some enthusiasm into our pursuits. Watching people winning cars and all expenses paid overseas 5-star holidays, hearing about the thousands that ordinary people now earn and how much their lives have changed can be the fire you need to rev up your personal engine. I have attended a number of these events and even if you never get to join, it may be worthwhile to purchase a ticket to one.

Even the network marketing company has multiple streams of income

It's important to understand the many streams of income that the network marketing company has so that you can make your decision wisely:

1. Your joining fee. That is a stream of income they project when they complete their financial statements. It may be a cost to you but to them it is an income stream.
2. All the non-salaried sales people they employ. In most companies, you are paid to work as a salesperson, but in the network marketing company you pay to work for the company. As you recruit your down-line, they also bring a joining fee and they add to the non-salaried workforce.
3. The products that you are selling and using for your own consumption.
4. The educational products that you are buying.
5. The sale of tickets to all their events.

6. The sponsorship and discounts they get on products and services because you and others who have joined have suddenly given them the muscle to negotiate for bulk purchases.

Why is it okay for you to have one or two income streams, if even the networking company you have joined has at least six streams? It may mean building one income stream at a time, but never lose sight of the big picture and do not get comfortable with making a lot of money from one income stream.

When I got fired from my job, my salary was my only established source of income and the one thing that kept me from the streets is the fact that I had already started establishing book sales, speaking and rental income as additional streams. At that time, I thought about all the other streams as side streams but losing my salary showed me that I should have focused on the other streams more. It's great to say I earn six figures and to keep climbing that one ladder but it may be wiser to focus on diversifying; it hedges your risk. We grew up being told not to put all our eggs in one basket and just in case we forgot why, here is a reminder: if that basket breaks then you will lose all your eggs.

14. Grow Money

There are so many vehicles to grow money, and there are businesses and entire cities that are built on the premise of growing money. The term growing can be misleading because it gives an impression that money is a living thing. We need to acknowledge that money can grow, because the person who doesn't know that money can grow will allow opportunities to pass him by every day. It's one thing to watch the money you have made increasing because of your efforts, but the money can also grow without you putting in additional effort if you are correctly informed about how to grow money.

Most of the passive income streams that we introduced provide one way to grow your money and you would do well to employ as many of them as you can. Parallel to passive income streams, we need to involve professionals to assist us with growing our money. There are people who spent their time at reputable institutions learning and practising how to grow money. In the same way that you wouldn't perform an operation on yourself or your loved ones if you are not a qualified doctor, you would do well to request assistance to grow your money. When most of us go for operations, we educate ourselves about the procedure, we do our own research, we ask questions and request for second and third opinions, we visit specialists, etc. In the same way, before you hand over your hard-earned money to anyone, do your own research, lest you pay for your ignorance with your hard-earned money. We all wish to become financial experts overnight, we want to read one book and have the science of growing money all figured out, but that is often just a dream. Be humble enough to know how far your finance education is and if you are not ready to buy your own shares or you don't have enough money to buy bonds on your own, joining a reputable firm may not be such a bad idea.

Brokers, financial planners, financial advisors, personal bankers, unit trusts, bonds, retirement annuities and so many more, are all an integral part of your journey to growing your money. Don't be afraid to involve any of these resources as part of your strategy, for many of us it may be the difference between losing and growing our money.

Think about money the way farmers think about their flocks. Your calf must grow to be a fully-grown cow, and then it must mate with a bull so that it can give birth to another calf. The farmer has two cows now that can mate and his flock can now increase to four. The farmer could have killed his one calf and sold the meat for a profit to the butchery, but if he allows the calf to live then he can enjoy the milk as the cow multiplies itself. The farmer will not eat meat though, but he can enjoy milk as he gives his flock a chance to grow. Think very clearly about your strategy to grow money. Can you live on milk, as you give your flock a chance to grow? Or are you in a hurry to eat meat now?

15. Conclusion

The power of this book is not in the information contained therein. The true power of this book is in you the reader. The question is what will you do to affect your finances? Which of these principles will you apply and how soon will you apply them? The wonderful thing about this book is that it is full of practical ideas that you can implement immediately.

I do hope you are encouraged to bring a lasting change to your finances. I hope you are now moved to design a personal finance system that includes getting out of debt, creating additional streams of income in your life, and maximising all the existing streams in your life.

The first step to succeeding with money is beginning to understand that there are principles that govern the art of making, keeping and growing money. In this first instalment of Money 101, we introduced you to some of these principles and the next instalment will go deeper into them.

16. About the author

Mantsha is a motivational speaker, author, blogger, mentor, pastor and a chemical engineer. She was born in Limpopo and she holds a BSc. Chemical Engineering degree from the University of Witwatersrand.

She began her career in the PGM Mining industry as an engineer and has vast experience in Government, Mining, Development Finance, Engineering, Management Consulting and Publishing.

Mantsha is the author of the following books: Single and Loving It, How to pray the word of God, Failure is not Final, How to realize your Personal Vision and Money 101.

She is a mentor and business coach and she is a publisher. Mantsha is passionate about development and runs several youth and women's programmes. "When excellence is on the stage it demands attention"

Mantsha is a regular speaker at conferences, events and churches. She is also the Senior Pastor of the Church of Jesus Christ in Midrand, South Africa.

Endnotes

Chapter 3. Busting the lies you believe about money

Detailed description of America's wealthy can be found in *The Millionaire Next Door: The Surprising Secrets of America's Wealthy* by Thomas J. Stanley, PhD and William Danko, PhD and published by RosettaBooks LLC, 2010.

Chapter 4. Create an abundance mentality

Detailed findings can be obtained in *The Millionaire Next Door: The Surprising Secrets of America's Wealthy* by Thomas J. Stanley, PhD and William Danko, PhD and published by RosettaBooks LLC, 2010.

Chapter 6. Design a personal money system

For a more detailed look at Dave Ramsey's system refer to his book: *The Total Money Makeover: A proven plan for financial fitness* by Dave Ramsey and published by Thomas Nelson, Inc, 2007.

For a more detailed look at George Clason's system refer to his book: *The Richest Man in Babylon* by George S. Clason and published by Magdalene Press, 2015.

For a more detailed look at Napoleon Hill's system refer to his book: *Think and Grow Rich by* Napoleon Hill, compiled by Ross Cornwell and published by Mindpower Press, 1926.

Chapter 8. Get out of DEBT

The Real Estate Investment Strategy is found in Kim Kiyosaki's book: *Rich Woman, A call for women* by Kim Kiyosaki and published by Rich Press, 2006.

Chapter 10. Find a Job

This chapter is based on the parable found in the chapter: The luckiest man in Babylon of the book: *The Richest Man in Babylon* by George S. Clason and published by Magdalene Press, 2015.

Chapter 12. Make Passive Income

See the detailed concept in Robert Kiyosaki's book: *Rich Dad Poor Dad, What The Rich Teach Their Children About Money That the Poor and Middle Class do not, by* Robert Kiyosaki and published by Plata Publishing LLC, 2011.

www.ingramcontent.com/pod-product-compliance
Lightning Source LLC
Chambersburg PA
CBHW031432210526
45464CB00005B/2165